H A M L Y N

FAVOURITE COOKBOOKS

International Cookery

Annette Wolter

Cover photograph by Chris Crofton

Published 1986
by Hamlyn Publishing,
a division of The Hamlyn Publishing Group Ltd
Bridge House, London Road, Twickenham, Middlesex, England

First published under the title
Specialitaten aus 30 Ländern
© Copyright by Gräfe und Unzer Verlag, München

ISBN 0 600 32625 X

Set in Monophoto Sabon
by Servis Filmsetting Ltd, Manchester, England
Printed in Italy

Contents

Useful facts and figures

Notes on metrication
In this book quantities are given in metric and Imperial measures. Exact conversion from Imperial to metric measures does not usually give very convenient working quantities and so the metric measures have been rounded off into units of 25 grams. The table below shows the recommended equivalents.

Ounces	Approx g to nearest whole figure	Recommended conversion to nearest unit of 25
1	28	25
2	57	50
3	85	75
4	113	100
5	142	150
6	170	175
7	198	200
8	227	225
9	255	250
10	283	275
11	312	300
12	340	350
13	368	375
14	396	400
15	425	425
16 (1 lb)	454	450
17	482	475
18	510	500
19	539	550
20 (1¼ lb)	567	575

Note: When converting quantities over 20 oz first add the appropriate figures in the centre column, then adjust to the nearest unit of 25. As a general guide, 1 kg (1000 g) equals 2.2 lb or about 2 lb 3 oz. This method of conversion give good results in nearly all cases, although in certain pastry and cake recipes a more accurate conversion is necessary to produce a balanced recipe.

Liquid measures The millilitre has been used in this book and the following table gives a few examples.

Imperial	Approx ml to nearest whole figure	Recommended ml
¼ pint	142	150 ml
½ pint	283	300 ml
¾ pint	425	450 ml
1 pint	567	600 ml
1½ pint	851	900 ml
1¾ pints	992	1000 ml (1 litre)

Spoon measures All spoon measures given in this book are level unless otherwise stated.

Can sizes At present, cans are marked with the exact (usually to the nearest whole number) metric equivalent of the Imperial weight of the contents, so we have followed this practice when giving can sizes.

Oven temperatures
The table below gives recommended equivalents.

	°C	°F	Gas Mark
Very cool	110	225	¼
	120	250	½
Cool	140	275	1
	150	300	2
Moderate	160	325	3
	180	350	4
Moderately hot	190	375	5
	200	400	6
Hot	220	425	7
	230	450	8
Very hot	240	475	9

Note: WHEN MAKING ANY OF THE RECIPES IN THIS BOOK, ONLY FOLLOW ONE SET OF MEASURES AS THEY ARE NOT INTERCHANGEABLE.

Introduction

Have you ever been curious about cooking in other countries? If so this book provides the ideal introduction for the beginner and experienced cook alike to sample the common dishes prepared in kitchens all over the world, as well as some of the internationally-known 'classics' such as Peking duck or Hungarian goulash. Gathered together here by Annette Wolter are a collection of recipes from all over the globe, ranging from Scandinavia to South Africa, Great Britain to China. There are dishes from over thirty countries included in the book, many of which are illustrated in colour.

Here are recipes suitable for every occasion. At lunchtime why not try the Aubergine omelette from Iran or the nourishing Thick chicken soup from Belgium. There is a wealth of choice for family meals such as the always popular Lasagne from Italy, or try the Minced beef bake from South Africa, which as well as being very tasty also provides an economical family dish.

When you have invited people to dinner and wish to have a formal or elaborate meal, why not make the Brazilian Creole shellfish soup or the French Home-made terrine followed by Duck with orange or Beef in lemon sauce? There are so many dishes which are suitable for entertaining that the only difficulty is deciding what to choose!

Desserts are not forgotten, either, and this book includes the delicious Zabaglione from Italy, Apple fritters from Belgium and the superb Cherry strudel from Austria.

Do experiment and try out some of the more unfamiliar dishes such as Stuffed corn pancakes from Mexico or Noodle stew from East Africa. An effort has been made to keep all the ingredients simple and accessible.

Note: Each recipe in this book will serve four people.

Italy

Neapolitan pizza
Pizza alla napoletana

For the dough
15 g/½ oz dried yeast
150 ml/¼ pint lukewarm milk or water
225 g/8 oz flour
1 egg, beaten
generous pinch of grated nutmeg
2 tablespoons oil or lard

For the topping
450 g/1 lb tomatoes
8 anchovy fillets
225 g/8 oz mozzarella cheese
4 tablespoons oil
generous pinch of salt and black pepper
generous pinch of oregano
generous pinch of dried thyme

Dissolve the yeast in the milk and leave for 10 minutes, until frothy. Sift the flour into a mixing bowl, make a well in the centre and stir in the dissolved yeast mixture. Work the flour into the yeast mixture with the egg, nutmeg and oil or lard to make a smooth, firm dough and leave to rise for 20 minutes.

Roll out the dough and line a greased, shallow, round, 30-cm/12-in baking tin. Peel the tomatoes (see below) and slice. Chop the anchovy fillets. Slice the cheese. Sprinkle the pizza base with oil. Arrange the sliced tomato, anchovies and cheese over the base, sprinkle with the salt, pepper and herbs and again with oil. Bake the pizza in a hot oven (220 C, 425 F, gas 7) for about 30 minutes.

Variations: Pizza bases (including ready-made bases) can be used with a variety of toppings: for example salami, ham, peeled cooked prawns, artichoke hearts, mushrooms, green pepper. Try seasoning with garlic, basil and Parmesan cheese.

To peel tomatoes: Place the tomatoes in a large bowl and pour in sufficient boiling water to cover them. Leave for 1 to 2 minutes, depending on the ripeness of the fruit, then drain. Peel at once, using a sharp knife to slit the skins and the rest should slide off easily

Spaghetti Bolognese
Spaghetti alla bolognese

a small piece of celeriac
3 tablespoons olive oil
2 onions, chopped
1 carrot, finely diced
1 clove garlic, crushed
1 bay leaf
1 teaspoon salt
225 g/8 oz minced beef
6 tablespoons dry white wine
450 g/1 lb spaghetti
4 tomatoes
1 tablespoon concentrated tomato purée
generous pinch of pepper
1 teaspoon paprika
50 g/2 oz Parmesan cheese, grated

Peel and wash the celeriac and cut into thin sticks. Heat the oil in a pan, add the onion, carrot, celeriac, garlic, bay leaf and a generous pinch of salt. Mix thoroughly. Add the meat and brown, stirring continuously. Add the white wine, cover the pan and simmer for about 20 minutes. Fold the spaghetti into a large pan of boiling salted water, stir once and boil for 15 to 20 minutes. Peel and finely chop the tomatoes (see below left) and add to the meat with the tomato purée, pepper and paprika. Stirring from time to time, cook the sauce until thick and smooth. Drain the spaghetti. Transfer to a heated bowl and top with the Bolognese sauce. Serve the grated Parmesan separately.

Neapolitan pizza and Spaghetti Bolognese

Lasagne with meat sauce

Lasagne al forno

450 g/1 lb lasagne
salt
450 g/1 lb veal
100 g/4 oz bacon
50 g/2 oz butter
1 small onion, finely chopped
1 carrot, finely diced
a small piece of celeriac, thinly sliced
450 g/1 lb peeled chopped tomatoes, canned or fresh
1 teaspoon flour
150 ml/¼ pint stock
150 ml/¼ pint red wine
½ teaspoon pepper
3 tablespoons finely chopped parsley
3 tablespoons finely chopped basil
175 g/6 oz Parmesan cheese, grated

Cook the lasagne in a large pan of salted water as instructed on the packet, until pliable but not too soft. Very finely dice the veal and bacon. Rinse the cooked lasagne in cold water and drain.

Completely brown the diced veal and bacon in the butter. Add the onion and fry until transparent. Add the carrot and celeriac and cook for about 2 minutes, stirring continuously. Stir in the tomatoes, sprinkle on the flour and stir in the stock and red wine. Cover the pan and simmer the meat sauce gently for 45 minutes. Finally, season with the pepper, parsley, basil and salt to taste. Grease a lasagne or soufflé dish and cover the base with lasagne. Cover with a layer of meat sauce, then another layer of lasagne and continue in this way until you have used up all the ingredients, finishing with a generous layer of meat sauce. Sprinkle with Parmesan cheese and bake in a moderately hot oven (200 C, 400 F, gas 6) until the cheese begins to brown.

Baked polenta

Polenta fritta

1 litre/2 pints water
½ teaspoon salt
100 g/4 oz butter
225 g/8 oz maize flour
100 g/4 oz Parmesan cheese, grated

Bring the water to the boil with the salt and half the butter. Stirring continuously, slowly sprinkle the maize flour into the hot liquid, continue stirring and then simmer over a low heat until you have a thick paste. Stir in the grated cheese. Rinse a flat porcelain dish or plate in cold water, spread the mixture over the dish and leave to cool for at least 1 hour. Cut the cold polenta into rectangles and then fry in the remaining butter until golden brown.

Sole fillets in Marsala

Sogliole al marsala

8 medium-sized sole fillets
2–3 tablespoons flour
100 g/4 oz butter
salt
4 tablespoons Marsala wine
2 teaspoons finely chopped parsley
a few drops of lemon juice

Coat the sole fillets generously in the flour and shake off any excess. Melt a quarter of the butter in a frying pan, add 4 fillets to the pan and salt to taste. Fry until golden brown on one side, turn, add 2 tablespoons Marsala and brown the other side of the fillets. Fry the remaining fillets in the same way. Arrange the cooked fillets on a heated plate and pour on the juices from the pan. Work the parsley into the remaining butter with a few drops of lemon juice. Dot knobs of parsley butter over the sole fillets and serve immediately.

Osso buco

900 g/2 lb knuckle of veal
2 teaspoons salt
2 tablespoons flour
4 onions
2 carrots
$\frac{1}{2}$ medium-sized celeriac
2 potatoes
3 tablespoons olive oil
150 ml/$\frac{1}{4}$ pint dry white wine
300 ml/$\frac{1}{2}$ pint tomato juice
1 teaspoon fresh or $\frac{1}{2}$ teaspoon dried rosemary
3 tablespoons finely chopped mixed herbs

Cut the veal into fairly large, equal slices. Season the veal with salt and coat in flour. Cut the onions into wedges. Cut the carrots into sticks. Peel, wash and dice the celeriac. Peel, wash and quarter the potatoes.

Heat the oil in a large pan and brown the veal well on both sides. Add the onions, carrots, celeriac and potatoes to the meat and fry, stirring frequently.

Osso buco

When everything is nice and brown, stir the wine and tomato juice into the cooking juices. Stir in the rosemary, cover the pan and braise for 1$\frac{1}{2}$ hours. Lift the meat out of the sauce and transfer to a heated plate. Stir the mixed herbs into the vegetable sauce and pour back over the veal.

Zabaglione

4 egg yolks
4 tablespoons caster sugar
150 ml/$\frac{1}{4}$ pint Marsala wine
juice of $\frac{1}{2}$ lemon

Whisk the egg yolks with the sugar, Marsala and lemon juice until frothy. Then whisk over a saucepan of hot water until light and creamy. Pour into four glass dishes, leave to cool slightly and serve immediately or serve chilled.

Spain

Paella

450 g/1 lb long-grain rice
2 tomatoes
225 g/8 oz each cooked chicken, veal and pork
3 tablespoons olive oil
1 large onion, diced
2 cloves garlic, crushed
450 g/1 lb canned mussels
12–16 peeled cooked prawns
½ teaspoon each salt, pepper, paprika, marjoram and thyme
2 tablespoons finely chopped parsley
1 tablespoon lemon juice
50 g/2 oz stuffed green olives
225 g/8 oz cooked peas
1 red pepper, deseeded and cut into strips
1 green pepper, deseeded and cut into strips

Boil the rice in a large pan of salted water until fluffy but not soft, tip into a sieve and drain. Cut the tomatoes into wedges. Cut the meat into equal-sized cubes.

Heat a little oil in a large frying pan. First add the onion, then the garlic and finally the tomatoes, and warm through. Add the diced meat and heat. Drain the mussels. Add the mussels and prawns to the pan and heat through, stirring from time to time. Add the rice with a little more oil and stir in thoroughly. Season with salt, pepper, paprika, marjoram, thyme, parsley and lemon juice. Slice the olives and add to the pan with the peas and peppers. Stir continuously until all the ingredients are piping hot. Serve straight from the pan.

Andalusian vegetable soup

Gazpacho andaluz

900 g/2 lb tomatoes
1 red pepper
1 small cucumber
2 cloves garlic, crushed
1 teaspoon salt
1 onion, finely chopped
250 g/8 fl oz water
5 tablespoons olive oil
3 tablespoons vinegar
generous pinch of black pepper
100 g/4 oz white bread, finely cubed
ice cubes (optional)

Peel, deseed and dice the tomatoes (see page 7). Halve the pepper, remove the seeds and pith, wash and finely dice. Peel and slice the cucumber and then cut the slices into cubes. Mix the garlic with the salt. Keep half the prepared vegetables to one side. Blend the remaining vegetables in a liquidiser or food processor with the garlic, water, olive oil, vinegar and pepper. Chill the blended vegetables in a covered bowl for 30 minutes.

To serve: Serve the diced vegetables and bread cubes in small bowls and serve the soup separately. The soup should be served well chilled, possibly with a few ice cubes floating on the top. At the table everyone helps themselves to soup, raw vegetables and bread cubes.

Paella

Kidneys in sherry

Riñones con jerez

675 g/1½ lb calf's kidney
salt and freshly ground black pepper
5 tablespoons olive oil
1 onion, finely chopped
1 clove garlic, crushed
1 tablespoon flour
150 ml/¼ pint beef stock
1 bay leaf
5 tablespoons dry sherry

Wash the kidneys thoroughly, cut in half length-ways, remove fat and blood vessels, thinly slice and season to taste. In a saucepan heat 4 tablespoons oil and fry the onion and garlic until transparent. Sprinkle on the flour, stir in the stock and add the bay leaf. Simmer for 4 minutes, stirring continuously, then remove the sauce from the heat. Heat the remaining oil in a frying pan and quickly brown the slices of kidney, turning them frequently. Take the bay leaf out of the sauce and add the kidney. Dilute the juices in the frying pan with the sherry, add to the kidneys and reheat. Serve immediately.

Green beans

Judias verdes

450 g/1 lb green beans
salt
5 tomatoes
4 tablespoons olive oil
2 cloves garlic, crushed
1 onion, finely chopped
2 tablespoons finely chopped thyme
3 tablespoons water
100 g/4 oz boiled ham

Trim and wash the beans and boil in salted water in an open pan for 15 minutes. Peel and finely chop the tomatoes (see page 7). Drain the beans. Heat the olive oil. Fry the garlic for about 2 minutes and then remove from the pan. Tip the chopped onion into the oil and add the beans. Add the chopped tomato, thyme and water and simmer for 15 minutes. Cut the ham into even strips and heat through with the beans for 5 minutes.

Flamenco eggs

175 g/6 oz green beans
100 g/4 oz rindless bacon
5 tablespoons olive oil
1 Spanish onion, diced
1 clove garlic, crushed
3 tomatoes
1 red pepper, deseeded and cut into strips
100 g/4 oz frozen peas
pinch each of salt, pepper and paprika
225 g/8 oz chorizo or salami, sliced
4 eggs

String the beans and cut into 5-cm/2-in lengths. Cut the bacon into strips. Heat the olive oil in a large frying pan and add the onion and garlic. Cook for a couple of minutes until they begin to brown. Peel, deseed and chop the tomatoes (see page 7) and add to the frying pan with the red pepper, peas and beans. Season to taste with the salt, pepper and paprika. Simmer over a gentle heat for 10 to 15 minutes.

Reserve 4 pieces of the chorizo or salami and add the rest to the pan. Add the bacon. Using a small ladle or spoon, make four indentations in the vegetable mixture and place an egg in each. Cover each egg with a slice of chorizo or salami. Bake in a moderately hot oven (200 C, 400 F, gas 6) for about 10 minutes or until the egg whites are firm.

Chicken pie

Empanada gallega

1 small chicken, cooked
1 yellow pepper, deseeded
1 green pepper, deseeded
15–20 stuffed olives
3 tomatoes
3 tablespoons olive oil
1 large onion, chopped
1 clove garlic, crushed
salt and black pepper
1 tablespoon finely chopped parsley
1 (368-g/13-oz) packet frozen puff pastry, defrosted
2 tablespoons flour
1 egg yolk

Remove the skin and bone from the chicken and cut up the meat. Cut the peppers into rings. Slice the olives. Peel and dice the tomatoes (see page 7).

Heat the oil in a saucepan and quickly fry the onion and garlic. Add the peppers, olives and tomatoes and fry with the onion. Add the chicken, season to taste and cook for a few minutes more. Finally add the parsley. Roll out the puff pastry thinly on a worktop sprinkled with the 2 tablespoons flour and line two small ovenproof dishes (about 20 cm/ 8 in. in diameter) or one large pie tin. Spread the filling over the pastry. Cover each pie with a pastry lid and pinch the edges together, moistening with a little water if necessary. Whisk the egg yolk and brush over the top of the pies. Bake the chicken pies in a hot oven (220 C, 425 F, gas 7) for 40 minutes.

Chicken pie

France

Marseilles fish soup
Bouillabaisse marseillaise

675 g/1½ lb assorted fish (mackerel, haddock,
cod, sole, halibut, pike, eel)
2 green peppers, deseeded
a small piece of celeriac
1 leek
4 tomatoes
about 4 tablespoons olive oil
4 cloves garlic
4 onions, finely chopped
1 teaspoon salt
1 carrot, sliced
225 g/8 oz fresh mussels, with beards removed
100 g/4 oz peeled cooked prawns
pinch of saffron powder

Cut any fins off the fish; gut and descale then trim
and wash inside and out. If you have bought fish
with heads, cook with the head. Finely chop the
peppers. Peel and wash the celeriac then cut into
strips. Wash the leek thoroughly and cut into
slices. Peel, deseed and dice the tomatoes (see
page 7).

Heat the olive oil in a large pan and fry the fish on
each side. Peel and chop the garlic and add to the
fish with the onion. Fry until the onion is transparent. Sprinkle with the salt. Add the chopped
peppers, celeriac, carrot, leek and tomatoes to the
fish. Add sufficient water to cover then add the
mussels and cook over a moderate heat for about
15 minutes. At the end of the cooking time discard
any mussels which have not opened. Break the
prawns into pieces. Add the prawns to the soup
with the saffron powder. Reheat the soup for 5
minutes, but do not boil again. Serve hot.

Duck with orange
Canard à l'orange

1 small oven-ready duck, with liver
salt and pepper
300 ml/½ pint water
6 oranges
2 teaspoons flour
50 g/2 oz butter
1 glass sherry

Wash the duck, pat dry and rub the inside with salt
and pepper.

Pour the water into a dripping pan and place under
the roasting rack. Place the duck on the rack and
roast in a hot oven (220 C, 425 F, gas 7) for about 1
hour until brown, basting from time to time with
juices in the tin. Meanwhile, thinly cut the rind
from 1 orange and cut the rind into thin strips.
Squeeze the juice of 4 oranges. Take the roasted
duck out of the oven and keep hot. Stir the orange
juice into the roasting juices, having skimmed off
the excess fat first. Work the flour into half the
butter and stir into the orange sauce until dissolved. Add the orange rind. Flavour the sauce
with the sherry and seasoning to taste. Work the
duck's liver into a pulp using a fork, stir in a little of
the sauce, pour the mixture into the sauce and
warm through. Peel the remaining orange. Slice
both this and the orange you peeled earlier and
heat in the remaining butter. Serve the orange slices
and the sauce with the duck.

Serve with: Unsweetened whipped cream and
fried potatoes.

Duck with orange

Quiche Lorraine

225 g/8 oz flour
100 g/4 oz butter
generous pinch of salt
150 g/5 oz Emmental cheese
150 g/5 oz lean bacon
½ teaspoon paprika
4 eggs
300 ml/½ pint single cream
pinch of pepper
2 tablespoons finely chopped parsley

Work together the flour, butter, salt and a little cold water to make a shortcrust pastry. Leave the pastry in the refrigerator for 1 hour. Finely dice the cheese. Finely dice the bacon, sprinkle with the paprika and fry, then leave to cool.

Roll out the pastry and use to line a 23-cm/9-in tin. Whisk the eggs with the cream and season with a pinch of salt and pepper. Gently stir in the cheese, bacon and parsley. Pour the mixture into the flan case. Place the flan in a moderately hot oven (200 C, 400 F, gas 6) for a few minutes and then reduce the oven to moderate (180 C, 350 F, gas 4). Bake the flan for a further 30 to 40 minutes, until golden brown.

To serve: Cut the flan like a cake and serve hot.

Variations: Quiche Lorraine is also delicious made with slices of Cheddar or Cheshire cheese. The flan case can be made with frozen puff pastry if preferred.

Chicken in wine

Coq au vin

4 rashers rindless streaky bacon
50 g/2 oz butter
2 small (450-g/1-lb) oven-ready chickens
salt and pepper
2 tablespoons brandy
600 ml/1 pint red wine (Burgundy, Beaujolais or Côte du Rhone)
about 150 ml/¼ pint chicken stock
1 clove garlic, crushed
¼ teaspoon thyme
1 bay leaf
8 shallots
225 g/8 oz button mushrooms
1 tablespoon oil
1 tablespoon flour
2 tablespoons finely chopped parsley

Cut the bacon into fine strips. Heat half the butter, fry the bacon until golden, remove from the pan and keep in reserve. Cut the chicken into portions, rinse in cold water and pat dry.

Fry the chicken pieces in the butter in which you fried the bacon until brown all over and season to taste. Return the bacon to the pan, cover and cook over a low heat for 10 minutes, turning the chicken once. Remove the lid and slowly pour the brandy over the chicken. Swirl the pan to distribute the brandy evenly. Add the red wine and sufficient stock to cover. Add the garlic to the pan with the thyme and bay leaf. Cover and cook over a moderate heat for 30 minutes. Peel and halve the shallots; trim and clean the mushrooms. Heat the oil and fry the shallots and mushrooms over a moderate heat for 15 minutes. Remove the chicken pieces from the first pan and keep hot. Continue cooking the sauce in the open pan until it has reduced to about 600 ml/1 pint. Melt the remaining butter, sprinkle in the flour, and stir until smooth. Remove the bay leaf from the sauce and stir in the butter and flour mixture. Add the chicken pieces, shallots and mushrooms to the sauce and reheat without allowing the sauce to boil. Sprinkle with the parsley and serve straight from the pan.

Quiche Lorraine

Peppered steaks

Steak au poivre

2 shallots
8 tablespoons butter
salt
4 fillet steaks
½ clove garlic
1 tablespoon white peppercorns
3 tablespoons brandy

Peel and very finely chop the shallots and work into 5 tablespoons butter with a pinch of salt. Shape the butter into a rectangle, cover and chill. Rub the steaks with the cut side of garlic and season with salt. Coarsely crush the peppercorns in a mortar, or crush by wrapping in a tea-towel and beating with a meat hammer. Work the pepper into 1 tablespoon butter. Spread the steaks thickly with this butter. Heat a frying pan and fry the steaks for 3 to 4 minutes each side in the remaining butter. Transfer to a warm plate. Stir the brandy into the juice in the pan and pour over the steaks. Top with the shallot butter.

Steak in red wine

Entrecôte marchand de vin

1 tablespoon butter
1 tablespoon oil
4 fillet or sirloin steaks
3 shallots
2 clove garlic, crushed (optional)
300 ml/½ pint red wine
3 tablespoons chopped parsley
salt and pepper

Heat the butter and oil in a large frying pan and fry the steaks for 3 to 4 minutes each side. Transfer to a warm plate. Peel and finely chop the shallots and add to the frying pan with the garlic, if using. Soften for a few minutes before pouring in the wine. Boil until the liquid has reduced by half then remove from the heat and add the parsley. Season to taste with salt and pepper then pour the sauce over the reserved steaks.

Peppered steaks

Home-made terrine

Terrine à la maison

275 g/10 oz lean pork
275 g/10 oz veal
25 g/1 oz fatty bacon
150 g/5 oz pig's liver
1 tablespoon finely chopped onion
1 clove garlic, crushed
2 tablespoons butter
100 g/4 oz chicken livers
2 tablespoons dry white wine
1 tablespoon brandy
2 egg yolks
1 teaspoon salt
$\frac{1}{2}$ teaspoon freshly ground black pepper
pinch each of dried thyme and marjoram
small pinch of ground allspice
150 g/5 oz thin rashers streaky bacon
1 small bay leaf

Finely mince the meat, fatty bacon and pig's liver. Fry the onion and garlic in half the butter until transparent, then remove from the pan. Add the remaining butter to the pan and fry the chicken livers for 1 to 2 minutes. Stir the onion mixture and all the ingredients from the wine to the allspice into the minced meat mixture. Line a small earthenware ovenproof dish with some of the bacon rashers. Place half the meat mixture in the dish and press down firmly. Cut the chicken livers into 1-cm/$\frac{1}{2}$-in cubes and spread over the meat mixture in the dish. Cover with the remaining minced meat and again press down well. Place the bay leaf on the top and cover with the remaining bacon rashers. Place the lid on the dish or cover tightly with aluminium foil. Place the dish in a roasting tin filled with 2.5 cm/1 in water in a moderate oven (180C, 350F, gas 4) and cook for about 1$\frac{1}{4}$ hours. Remove the lid or foil and leave the terrine to cool in the oven before transferring to the refrigerator. Leave for at least 24 hours before serving.

Chocolate mousse

Mousse au chocolat

4 eggs, separated
3 tablespoons caster sugar
2 tablespoons brandy
175 g/6 oz plain chocolate
3 tablespoons strong coffee
100 g/4 oz butter
whipped cream to decorate

Whisk the egg yolks with the sugar until frothy. Add the brandy and whisk over a pan of boiling water for 5 minutes until hot. Then transfer the bowl to a large dish full of ice cubes and whisk until cool. Warm the chocolate with the coffee in a bowl over a basin of hot water, stirring continuously until the chocolate has melted. Cut the butter into small flakes and stir in. Whisk the egg whites until stiff. Fold the chocolate mixture into the egg yolks and then gradually fold in the whites. Transfer the mousse to a glass dish and leave in the refrigerator to set. Decorate with whipped cream.

Home-made terrine
Chocolate mousse

Switzerland

Basle brown soup

50 g/2 oz butter
4 tablespoons flour
1 onion, finely chopped
1 piece bacon rind
1 litre/2 pints beef stock
150 ml/$\frac{1}{4}$ pint red wine
100 g/4 oz Gruyère or Emmental cheese,
grated, to serve

Melt the butter, cook the flour in the butter until golden, add the onion and cook until transparent. Add the bacon rind and gradually stir in the stock. Whisk the soup vigorously until it comes to the boil and then simmer for 30 minutes. Strain the soup and stir in the red wine.

To serve: Serve the grated cheese separately to be sprinkled into the soup at the table.

Zurich rösti

675 g/1$\frac{1}{2}$ lb potatoes, boiled in their skins the
day before
5 tablespoons oil
1 teaspoon salt
2 tablespoons butter

Peel and slice the potatoes. Heat the oil in a large frying pan, add the potatoes, sprinkle with salt and brown over a moderate heat without stirring. While the underside is cooking spread the butter over the surface. Press the potatoes together, using a fish slice or wooden spatula, to make a solid cake. Cook the underside until brown and crusty. Transfer the rösti to a plate, brown side uppermost. Serve very hot.

Serve with: Zurich chopped veal.

Zurich chopped veal

450 g/1 lb veal
225 g/8 oz mushrooms
about 2 tablespoons flour
50 g/2 oz butter
1 onion, chopped
150 ml/$\frac{1}{4}$ pint dry white wine
150 ml/$\frac{1}{4}$ pint single cream
salt and white pepper

The veal should be cut into extremely thin slices and you can either do this yourself or get the butcher to do it for you. Clean and thinly slice the mushrooms. Dip the slices of veal in the flour. Melt the butter in a frying pan and fry the onion until transparent. Add the veal and mushrooms and fry quickly over a high heat, stirring continuously. When the meat has browned stir in the wine and simmer to reduce. Then add the cream. Season to taste and stir through. Serve at once or the meat will become tough.

Serve with: Zurich rösti.

Cook's tip: To freeze, omit the cream and add it once defrosted.

Zurich chopped veal and Zurich rösti

Potée vaudoise

675 g/1½ lb leeks
40 g/1½ oz butter or margarine
1 onion, finely chopped
300 ml/½ pint beef stock
675 g/1½ lb potatoes
600 ml/1 pint dry white wine
4 smoked sausages, sliced
generous pinch of pepper

Trim and wash the leeks and cut into 2.5-cm/1-in lengths. Heat the butter or margarine and fry the onion until transparent. Add the leeks and fry, stirring occasionally. Then add the stock and simmer over a moderate heat for about 15 minutes. Cut the potatoes into large cubes. Add to the leeks and cook for 10 minutes. If necessary add a little water, but bear in mind the liquid should be almost completely evaporated by the end of the cooking time. Then add the wine, top with the sausages, cover the pan and simmer gently over a low heat for a further 20 minutes. Finally season with pepper to taste.

Bernese cheese soufflé

Ramequin

4 tablespoons butter or margarine
8 slices white bread
3–4 tablespoons brandy
4 eggs, separated
225 g/8 oz Emmental cheese, grated
150 ml/¼ pint cream
½ teaspoon salt
¼ teaspoon pepper
generous pinch of grated nutmeg

Grease a soufflé dish with 1 tablespoon butter or margarine. Cut the crusts off the bread. Heat the remaining fat and fry the bread on both sides. Layer the bread in the soufflé dish and sprinkle with the brandy. Beat the egg yolks with the cheese, cream, salt, pepper and nutmeg. Whisk the whites until stiff and fold into the yolk and cheese mixture. Pour over the bread and bake in a moderately hot oven (200 C, 400 F, gas 6) for 30 to 40 minutes.

Cheese fondue

1 small French loaf
½ clove garlic
150 ml/¼ pint dry white wine
10 oz/275 g Gruyère cheese, grated
10 oz/275 g Emmental cheese, grated
1 tablespoon cornflour
3 tablespoons kirsch
salt and freshly ground white pepper
pinch of freshly ground nutmeg (optional)

Cut the bread into bite-sized pieces without removing the crust. Rub the inside of a fondue pot with the cut side of the garlic clove. Pour the wine into the pan and heat gently. Gradually add the grated Gruyère and Emmental and stir well until the cheese has melted. Blend the cornflour and kirsch together and add to the fondue. Cook gently for 2 to 3 minutes then season to taste with salt, pepper and nutmeg (if using).

To serve: Place the cheese mixture over a spirit lamp on the table. Stick the chunks of bread onto forks, dip into the fondue and stir round well to coat.

Serve with: A selection of pickled vegetables such as gherkins, cucumber and onion. Raw vegetables are also a very good accompaniment to a cheese fondue – chunks of deseeded red, green and yellow pepper (with the pith removed) add colour and sticks of celery, cauliflower florets, cubes of carrots and slices of apple give a very good crisp texture. Another variation is to use cubed pieces of garlic sausage, cervelat, salami or cooked pork or beef sausages. If feeling extravagant you could try peeled cooked prawns or scampi (Dublin Bay prawns) to dip into the fondue.

Palatine-style venison

Pfälzer Hirschkeule

1 kg/2 lb leg of young venison
1 teaspoon salt
10 peppercorns
10 juniper berries
1 bay leaf
300 ml/½ pint red wine
100 g/4 oz rashers streaky bacon
50 g/2 oz fat
6 tablespoons cranberry sauce
6 tablespoons double cream
2 tablespoons flour
225 g/8 oz small chanterelles, fresh or canned,
or mushrooms
½ onion
1 tablespoon butter
1 tablespoon finely chopped parsley
salt and white pepper
milk (as required)

Lightly prick the skin of the venison and peel off, but take care not to pierce the meat itself or you will lose the juice. Place the meat in a bowl and add the salt, peppercorns, juniper berries, bay leaf and red wine. Marinate for 1 hour, turning the meat twice during this time.

Take the meat out of the marinade, wipe dry and cover with the bacon rashers. In a roasting tin heat the fat, place the meat in the tin and roast on the middle shelf of a moderately hot oven (200 C, 400 F, gas 6) for 1 hour. Whisk together thoroughly the cranberry sauce, cream and flour or blend for 1 minute in a liquidiser or food processor. Trim and wash the fresh chanterelles (or mushrooms) or drain canned ones. Very finely chop the onion. Heat the butter and fry the onion until transparent, then add the chanterelles and parsley. Cover the pan and simmer for 5 to 10 minutes. Season to taste. When the venison is cooked take it out of the roasting tin and keep hot. Stir the cranberry sauce into the roasting juices and cook to thicken. If the sauce becomes too thick add a little water or milk. Remove the bay leaf from the marinade and add the marinade to the sauce. Bring to the boil and strain. Remove the bacon from the meat, carve the meat, garnish with the chanterelles and serve with the sauce.

Serve with: Brussels sprouts, tomatoes and pasta. Alternatively serve with fresh new potatoes or baked potatoes with lightly cooked broccoli or green beans. Red cabbage is a traditional accompaniment to this dish. Cranberry or redcurrant sauce or jelly can also be served as a side sauce as well as being a major ingredient of the hot sauce which is served with the venison.

Palatine-style venison

Liver dumpling soup

Leberknödelsuppe

225 g/8 oz pig's or ox liver
4 bread rolls
50 g/2 oz bacon
1 large onion, chopped
2 eggs, beaten
1 teaspoon salt
2 tablespoons finely chopped parsley
½ teaspoon marjoram
breadcrumbs (as required)
1 litre/2 pints beef stock

Get your butcher to mince the liver or mince it finely yourself. Soak the rolls in water. Chop the bacon and fry with the onion. Squeeze the excess moisture from the rolls and mix with the onion and bacon, minced liver, eggs, salt, parsley and marjoram. Make one dumpling to test the consistency and simmer in hot water. If the dumpling falls apart work breadcrumbs into the mixture and then shape into dumpling. Bring the stock to the boil. Add the dumplings and simmer for about 15 minutes.

Bavarian leg of pork

Bayerische Schweinshaxe

1 leg fresh pork
1 teaspoon salt   ½ teaspoon black pepper
1 large onion
1 carrot
150 ml/¼ pint boiling water
½ teaspoon caraway seeds
3 peppercorns

Wash the pork, wipe dry and rub with the salt and pepper. Quarter the onion. Coarsely chop the carrot. Pour the water into a roasting tin and add the onion, carrot, caraway seeds and peppercorns. Place the pork in a moderate oven (180 C, 350 F, gas 4) on a rack over the roasting tin and roast for 1½ hours. Baste the pork from time to time with the sauce in the roasting tin. Cook until the pork is brown and crisp.

Serve with: Dumplings made from raw potato and cabbage salad.

Rhenish marinated beef

Rheinischer Sauerbraten

675 g/1½ lb brisket of beef
1 bunch soup vegetables (carrot, leek and celeriac)
1 onion
4 peppercorns
2 bay leaves
4 juniper berries
3 cloves
450 ml/¾ pint water
250 ml/8 fl oz wine vinegar
50 g/2 oz butter
piece of bacon rind
salt and pepper
2 tablespoons flour
250 ml/8 fl oz soured cream
75 g/3 oz raisins
3 tablespoons red wine

Wash the meat and place in a large casserole with a lid (earthenware, porcelain or glass). Chop the soup vegetables and quarter the onion. Bring the soup vegetables, onion, peppercorns, bay leaves, juniper berries and cloves to the boil in the water and vinegar. Leave to cool and pour over the brisket. Cover the casserole and leave the meat to marinate for two to three days, turning it from time to time.

Heat the butter in a stewpan. Dry the meat thoroughly and brown well in the hot butter. Add a little of the marinade and the bacon rind and season to taste. Cover the pan and braise for about 2 hours. Take the brisket out of the pan and keep hot. Strain the gravy from the meat and add sufficient water to make 600 ml/1 pint. Beat the flour into the soured cream, stir into the gravy and bring to the boil. Add the raisins and wine. Carve the meat and serve with the sauce.

Serve with: Potato dumplings (made either with cooked potato or half cooked, half raw potato), dried fruit or apple sauce.

Smoked pork fillet

Kasseler Rippenspeer

675 g/1½ lb piece smoked pork fillet
600 ml/1 pint boiling water
1 onion
1 carrot
1 bay leaf
2 peppercorns
1 teaspoon cornflour
300 ml/½ pint red wine
150 ml/¼ pint soured cream
salt and pepper

Wash and dry the meat and place, fat side undermost, in a roasting tin. Pour on the boiling water. Quarter the onion and chop the carrot. Add the onion, carrot, bay leaf and peppercorns to the tin and roast in a moderately hot oven (200 C, 400 F, gas 6) for 30 minutes. Then turn the meat over and roast for a further 30 minutes, basting frequently with the gravy in the tin. Transfer the meat to a warm plate and keep hot. Dilute the cooking juices with a little water and strain into a saucepan. Dissolve the cornflour in the red wine and stir into the sauce. Bring to the boil and then stir in the soured cream and season to taste with salt and pepper.

Serve with: Sauerkraut and boiled potatoes. The sauce can be served separately, as shown below, or poured over the pork fillet just before serving.

Smoked pork fillet

Belgium and Netherlands

Eel soup

Palingsoep – Netherlands

450 g/1 lb medium-sized fresh eels
about 1 litre/2 pints water
1 teaspoon salt
50 g/2 oz capers
3 tablespoons finely chopped parsley
50 g/2 oz butter
50 g/2 oz flour
pinch of white pepper
juice of $\frac{1}{2}$ lemon
$\frac{1}{2}$ teaspoon sugar
150 ml/$\frac{1}{4}$ pint dry white wine
1 egg yolk
4 tablespoons cream

Get the fishmonger to skin and cut up the eels. Wash the pieces well in cold water and then bring to the boil with the water and salt. Simmer for 15 minutes, until cooked, and leave to cool. Remove the eel from the water. Add the capers and parsley to the water and bring to the boil. Work the flour into the butter, dissolve in the eel water and return to the boil. Add the pieces of eel to the soup and reheat. Season with the pepper, lemon juice, sugar and white wine. Beat the egg yolk into the cream, stir into the soup and remove immediately from the heat.

Apple potato with chops and sausages

Heete bliksem – Netherlands

675 g/1$\frac{1}{2}$ lb potatoes
675 g/1$\frac{1}{2}$ lb cooking apples
3–4 onions
600 ml/1 pint beef stock
2 teaspoons white pepper
4 boneless pork chops
2–3 tablespoons lard
salt
4 pork sausages

Peel the potatoes and apples. Core the apples and cut into wedges. Cut the potatoes into similar-sized pieces. Slice the onions into rings.

Heat the stock. Add the potato and apple and cook until they fall. You may find you have to mash them in the end. Season generously with pepper. Fry the chops in the lard for 5 to 6 minutes each side until brown. Then season with salt. Fry the sausages and finally the onion rings.

To serve: Pile the potato and apple mixture in the middle of a plate. Top with the fried onion and surround with the chops and sausages.

Eel soup

Apple potato with chops and sausages

Apple fritters

Belgium

5 tablespoons flour
pinch of salt
1 tablespoon oil
1 egg and 2 egg whites
1 teaspoon rum
about 250 ml/8 fl oz light ale
450 g/1 lb apples
oil for deep frying
icing sugar to dust

Sift together the flour and salt then add the oil, 1 egg and the rum. Gradually beat in enough light ale to make a creamy batter. Cover and leave to stand for 1 hour.

Whisk the egg whites until stiff and fold into the batter. Peel, core and cut the apples into slices. Heat the oil to 180 C/350 F and deep fry the apple slices which have first been dipped in the batter. Fry 2 or 3 slices at a time until golden brown. Drain on absorbent kitchen paper and keep warm. When all the fritters have been cooked, sprinkle generously with icing sugar and serve while still hot.

Chicory with ham

Chicons au jambon – Belgium

8 small head chicory
salt
8 small slices uncooked ham
3 tablespoons butter
2 tablespoons flour
300 ml/½ pint hot milk
pinch of freshly grated nutmeg
50 g/2 oz cheese, grated

Trim and wash the chicory and cut off the root end. Cut a wedge out of the stalk end. Boil the chicory in water with a generous pinch of salt for 30 minutes. Drain the chicory and wrap each head in a slice of ham. Place in a greased baking dish. Set the grill or oven at very hot (240 C, 475 F, gas 9). Melt the butter in a saucepan, sprinkle in the flour and stir until golden. Add the hot milk with a pinch of salt and nutmeg and stir continuously to make a thick white sauce. Pour the sauce over the chicory in the dish. Sprinkle with the grated cheese and brown under the grill or in the oven for about 10 minutes until golden brown.

Thick chicken soup

Waterzooi de poulet – Belgium

2 small boiling fowl, with crop and heart
1 head celery
4 carrots
2 onions
3 peppercorns
2 cloves
1 teaspoon salt
about 1.5 litres/2¾ pints water
2 leeks
100 g/4 oz butter
40 g/1½ oz flour
2 eggs
6 tablespoons single cream

Bone the chicken and cut the meat into bite-sized pieces. Cut off the base of the celery, separate the sticks, wash thoroughly and cut up. Halve the carrots and then quarter each half lengthways. Quarter the onions.

Place the chicken with the wings, crop and heart in a saucepan. Add the celery, carrot, onion, peppercorns, cloves and salt, pour on the water and cook over a low heat for 50 to 60 minutes. Halve the leeks lengthways, wash thoroughly and cut into thin slices. Cook the leeks in a pan in 25 g/1 oz butter. Strain the chicken soup into the leek pan. Work the flour into the remaining butter, dissolve in the chicken soup and boil up several times. Skin the cooked chicken. Dice the cooked vegetables and return both to the soup. Beat the eggs with the cream, stir into the soup and remove immediately from the heat.

Brussels-style mussels

Moules à la bruxelloise – Belgium

3 kg/6½ lb fresh mussels
oatmeal
1 onion
40 g/1½ oz butter
sprig of celeriac leaves
150 ml/¼ pint dry white wine
pinch each of salt and pepper
1 bunch parsley
6 tablespoons single cream

Place the mussels in a large bowl or bucket of salted water with a handful of oatmeal and leave overnight. Drain then scrub the mussels thoroughly. Discard any that are not tightly closed, remove the beards by tugging strongly and then drain again in a colander. Finely chop the onion.

Melt the butter in a large, shallow saucepan and add the celeriac leaves, onion, wine, salt and pepper. Add the mussels to the pan, cover with the lid and cook over a high heat for 5 to 6 minutes. Chop the parsley. When the mussels have opened add the parsley and cream. Discard any mussels which have not opened.

Fried herrings

Hollandsenieuwe – Netherlands

4 herrings, gutted
salt and freshly ground pepper
2 tablespoons flour
4 tablespoons oil

Clean the herrings thoroughly inside and out under cold running water. Pat dry with absorbent kitchen paper. Season the fish inside and out with salt and pepper then dip in the flour, shaking off any excess.

Heat the oil in a large frying pan and cook the herrings for about 6 minutes on each side.

Brussels-style mussels

Great Britain

Cock-a-leekie soup

4 fairly thin leeks
1 small oven-ready boiling fowl, about 1 kg/2 lb
4 tablespoons pearl barley
1 litre/1¾ pints water
300 ml/½ pint chicken stock
generous pinch of salt
10 white peppercorns
1 bay leaf
pinch of freshly grated nutmeg

Trim and wash the leeks, remove any dark-green leaves and then cut into diagonal slices.

Place the chicken, leeks and pearl barley in a saucepan. Add the water, stock, salt, peppercorns and bay leaf and bring to the boil. Reduce the heat, skim off any scum, cover the pan and cook the chicken for about 2 hours. Skim off the fat. Remove the chicken from the pan, loosen the meat from the bones and cut the flesh into small pieces. Remove the peppercorns and bay leaf. Return the chicken meat to the soup, reheat and season to taste with the nutmeg.

Roast beef

1 kg/2 lb roasting beef (e.g. sirloin or rib)
salt and freshly ground black pepper
a little oil
1 onion
1 tomato (optional)

Rub the beef with salt and pepper. Brush a roasting grid with oil, place the beef fat side uppermost on the grid and place in a hot oven (230 C, 450 F, gas 8). Place a roasting tin containing 1 cm/½ in water under the beef. Quarter the onion and place in the roasting tin. You can also add a sliced tomato if you wish. Roast the beef for 50 to 60 minutes, turning the oven down to moderately hot (190 C, 375 F, gas 5) after the first 15 minutes. Turn off the oven and leave the beef for 10 minutes before taking it out of the oven. Serve with a gravy made from the juices in the roasting tin.

Yorkshire pudding

100 g/4 oz flour
½ teaspoon salt
2 eggs
300 ml/½ pint milk
2 tablespoons fat from roast beef tin or butter

Mix together the flour, salt, eggs and half the milk to make a batter and beat until smooth and light, gradually adding the remaining milk. Cover the bowl and leave to stand for 30 minutes.

Grease a deep oven dish or pudding tin – or individual deep tins – with the fat or butter. Pour the batter into the tin and bake on the top shelf of a hot oven (220 C, 425 F, gas 7) for about 25 minutes, until well risen and golden brown. If using individual tins the pudding should take only 15 to 20 minutes to cook. Cut up the pudding as if cutting a cake.

Serve with: Roast beef (recipe alongside).

Gravy

600 ml/1 pint beef stock
salt and freshly ground pepper
2–3 tablespoons wine (optional)
1 tablespoon cornflour (optional)

Skim the fat from the roasting juices of the tin in which the beef was cooked and add the hot stock. Season to taste with salt and pepper and stir in the wine, if using. To make a thick gravy dissolve the cornflour in 3 tablespoons cold water and stir into the gravy.

Steak and kidney pie

575 g/1¼ lb stewing steak
225 g/8 oz ox or lambs' kidneys
1 onion
½ teaspoon salt
½ teaspoon freshly ground black pepper
3 tablespoons flour
2 tablespoons melted suet or butter
350 ml/12 fl oz water
6 tablespoons dry sherry
1 tablespoon finely chopped parsley
a dash of Worcestershire sauce
1 (212-g/7½-oz) packet frozen puff pastry,
defrosted
1 egg yolk
1 tablespoon milk

Cut the meat into small cubes. Remove any fat and blood vessels from the kidneys and cut into similar-sized cubes. Wipe the beef and kidney dry. Chop the onion. Season the flour with salt and pepper and use to thoroughly coat the diced meat. Heat the suet and fry the onion until transparent. Add the meat and brown. Transfer this meat mixture to a casserole dish. Warm the water, stir in the sherry, parsley and Worcestershire sauce and pour over the meat. Cook for 2 to 3 hours in a moderate oven (160 C, 325 F, gas 3), until the meat is tender. Allow to cool slightly then transfer the mixture to a deep pie dish or tin. Roll out the pastry and cover the meat in the dish. Press the edges onto the dish and make a hole in the centre to allow the steam to escape. Use any excess pastry to make decorations for the pie crust. Beat the egg yolk with the milk and brush onto the pie crust. Bake the pie in a hot oven (220 C, 425 F, gas 7) for 30 minutes or until the pastry has puffed out and is a golden brown.

Baked Cod

75 g/3 oz butter
1 onion, finely chopped
50 g/2 oz button mushrooms, sliced
½ teaspoon fresh or ¼ teaspoon dried thyme
4 (225-g/8-oz) cod fillets or steaks
1 bay leaf
salt and pepper
40 g/1½ oz flour
1 pint milk
4 rashers rindless bacon
3 tablespoons dry breadcrumbs
parsley sprigs to garnish

Melt 25 g/1 oz butter and fry the onion and mushrooms. Place on the base of a baking dish and sprinkle on the thyme. Add the bay leaf. Arrange the cod fillets on top of the onion and mushrooms and season with the salt and pepper.

Make a white sauce by melting the remaining butter then adding the flour to make a roux. Gradually pour on the milk, stirring continuously. Pour the sauce over the fish and bake in a moderate oven (180 C, 350 F, gas 4) for 10 minutes.

Fry the bacon until crisp. Sprinkle the breadcrumbs over the fish, top with the bacon and brown for a further 10 minutes in a hot oven (220 C, 425 F, gas 7). Garnish with sprigs of parsley.

Steak and kidney pie

Christmas pudding

450 g/1 lb currants
225 g/8 oz raisins
225 g/8 oz sultanas
150 ml/¼ pint brandy
grated rind and juice of 1 orange and 1 lemon
100 g/4 oz candied lemon peel
100 g/4 oz candied orange peel
100 g/4 oz blanched almonds
225 g/8 oz white breadcrumbs
150 g/5 oz flour
¼ teaspoon each cinnamon, ground cloves and
ground ginger
generous pinch of grated nutmeg
1 teaspoon salt
225 g/8 oz shredded beef suet
5 eggs
225 g/8 oz soft brown sugar
2–3 tablespoons butter
3 tablespoons brandy to serve

Carefully sort the currants, raisins and sultanas, then soak in the brandy, orange and lemon juice overnight. Finely chop the candied lemon and orange peel. Chop the blanched almonds. Tip the breadcrumbs and flour into a bowl. Sprinkle the cinnamon, cloves, ginger, nutmeg and salt over the flour. Add the soaked fruit mixture, the suet and the grated rind of the orange and lemon. Mix together well. Gradually work in the eggs, stirring continuously. Finally add the sugar and mix very thoroughly.

Grease two pudding basins with the butter. Divide the mixture, which should be quite firm, between the two basins leaving about 5 cm/2 in at the top of each to allow for the puddings to rise. Cover the tops with greased greaseproof paper and a piece of greased aluminium foil pleated to allow for the puddings to rise. Stand each basin in a deep pan with enough boiling water to come about half way up the basin. Cook for 7 hours over a constant heat. You will have to keep topping up the pan with boiling water as the puddings cook. Leave the puddings to cool in the water and then store in the basins for at least one but preferably two weeks in a cool place, but not in the refrigerator. On the day the pudding is to be eaten boil the puddings for another 2 hours and then turn out onto a warm plate.

To serve: Warm the brandy, pour over the pudding, ignite and carry the flaming Christmas pudding to the table.

Cook's tip: Since Christmas puddings will keep for up to a year in a cool place, it is worth making this quantity of mixture even for a small family.

Crown roast with mint sauce

4 tablespoons finely chopped fresh mint
2 tablespoons sugar
5 tablespoons wine vinegar
2 tablespoons water
a little sherry
2 racks lamb cutlets, with about 5 cutlets
each side
1 clove garlic
1 teaspoon salt
350 ml/12 fl oz lamb stock, made from a
stock cube
a dash of Worcestershire sauce
2 tablespoons butter

Mix the chopped mint with the sugar. Bring the wine vinegar to the boil with the water and pour over the mint. Add a dash of sherry, cover and chill. Get your butcher to saw along the middle of the cutlets and to make a 2.5-cm/1-in cut between each cutlet. Remove the fatty skin from the racks. Finely chop the garlic and crush with the salt using the blade of a knife. Rub into the meat. Bend each row of cutlets into a semi-circle with the skin side innermost and tie both racks together to make a crown using kitchen string. Wipe the tops of the bones clean and wrap in aluminium foil. Place the crown in a roasting tin, pour in 250 ml/8 fl oz hot stock and roast in a moderately hot oven (190 C, 375 F, gas 5) for about 1¼ hours. Add a little more stock from time to time as necessary. Work the Worcestershire sauce into the butter and spread between the cutlets 10 minutes before the end of the cooking time.

To serve: Remove the foil and string from the crown roast, place paper cutlet frills on the top of the bones and served with the chilled mint sauce.

Christmas pudding

Schmolz herrings

Smaltsill – Sweden

8 salted herring fillets
6 potatoes
$\frac{1}{2}$ teaspoon salt
2 eggs
1 bunch radishes
1 tablespoon butter
4 tablespoons finely chopped parsley

Soak the herring fillets in water overnight to get rid of some of their saltiness. Wash, peel and halve the potatoes and boil in salted water for 10 minutes. Hard boil the eggs for 10 minutes. Rinse the herrings under cold water, pat dry and cut into diagonal strips, 1 cm/$\frac{1}{2}$ in wide. Place the strips of herring on a plate, place the plate over the boiling potatoes and heat over the potatoes for the remaining cooking time – about 15 minutes. Shell and coarsely chop the hard-boiled eggs. Wash and slice the radishes. Heat the butter in a saucepan until golden brown.

Surround the herring with the chopped parsley, sliced radishes and chopped egg and pour on the hot butter. Serve the potatoes separately.

Rissoles

Frikadeller – Denmark

1 onion
3 tablespoons flour
225 g/8 oz each minced veal and pork
1 tablespoon breadcrumbs
300 ml/$\frac{1}{2}$ pint soda water
1 egg
$\frac{1}{2}$ teaspoon salt
pinch of white pepper
1 tablespoon finely chopped parsley
3 tablespoons lard or butter

Very finely chop the onion. Work the flour into the meat. Add the breadcrumbs together with the soda water, a little at a time. Then mix in the egg, salt, pepper, parsley and chopped onion. Beat the mixture very well, cover tightly and chill for 30 minutes in the refrigerator. Shape the mixture into long rissoles and fry in the lard or butter one at a time for 7 to 8 minutes, turning once until cooked through and brown on the outside.

Serve with: Boiled potatoes and pickled beetroot or red cabbage.

Crayfish in dill

Keitetyt ravut – Finland

3.5 litres/6 pints water
2 tablespoons salt
4 tablespoons dill seeds
4 bunches fresh dill
30 freshwater crayfish

Bring the water to the boil in a very large pan with the salt, dill seeds and 2 bunches of the fresh dill and simmer for 10 minutes. Wash the crayfish thoroughly under cold running water. Place the crayfish in the boiling water five at a time, waiting each time for the water to return to the boil before adding the next five. Once all are in the pan, cover the pan and boil for 10 minutes. Place the remaining fresh dill in a large bowl. Lift the crayfish out of the pan on a skimmer and arrange over the dill. Strain the cooking water over the crayfish, cover the bowl and leave to cool at room temperature, then chill for several hours in the refrigerator. To serve remove the crayfish from the water.

Serve with: White bread and butter.

Crayfish in dill

Jutland-style haddock

Jutlander Schellfisch – Denmark

1 whole haddock, weighing about 1.5 kg/3 lb,
gutted and with head removed
juice of 1 lemon
1 teaspoon salt
100 g/4 oz streaky bacon
1 potato
2 teaspoons oil
2 tablespoons finely chopped dill
5 tablespoons grated Danbo (or Emmental)
cheese

Wash the haddock well, pat dry, sprinkle with lemon juice and leave to stand for 20 minutes.

Salt the fish inside and out. Cut the bacon into narrow strips 5 cm/2 in long and insert in two rows along the back of the fish. Peel the potato and place in the stomach cavity to hold the fish upright. Grease a baking dish with the oil. Place the haddock in the dish and bake in a hot oven (220 C, 425 F, gas 7) for 20 to 30 minutes. Shortly before the end of the cooking time sprinkle with dill. A few minutes later sprinkle the fish generously with the grated cheese and return to the oven to brown.

Serve with: Green beans with bacon and caraway potatoes.

Marinated salmon with mustard sauce

Gravlax med sas – Sweden

1–1.5 kg/2–3 lb fresh salmon (middle-cut)
4–5 bunches fresh dill
2 tablespoons coarse salt
5 tablespoons sugar
1 tablespoon white peppercorns
4 tablespoons strong prepared mustard
1 teaspoon mustard powder
2 tablespoons white wine vinegar
3 tablespoons oil
lemon wedges to garnish

Descale the salmon, cut it through lengthways and remove the bones if the fishmonger has not already done this for you.

Place one of the salmon fillets skin side underneath in a large glass, enamel or stainless steel bowl. Wash 3 or 4 bunches dill, shake dry and lay on the fish. Mix the salt with 3 tablespoons sugar and the coarsely ground peppercorns. Spread on the salmon and top with the second salmon fillet (skin side uppermost). Cover with aluminium foil. Place on top a wooden board, small enough to fit in the bowl, and weight down (with weights, rocks or cans) so the salmon is really under pressure. Marinate the salmon for at least two to three days, turning it over every 12 hours and spooning the resulting juice onto and between the fillets. To make the sauce mix the mustard with the mustard powder, the remaining sugar and the vinegar. Stir in the oil a few drops at a time to give a creamy sauce. Finely chop the remaining dill and fold in. Wipe the salmon dry before serving.

To serve: Place the salmon on its skin on a flat dish and, using a sharp knife, cut the thinnest slices possible. Garnish with lemon wedges. Serve with the mustard sauce.

Jutland-style haddock
Marinated salmon with mustard sauce

Consommé with bone marrow

Markschöberlsuppe

75 g/3 oz beef marrow
2 eggs
$\frac{1}{2}$ teaspoon salt
$\frac{1}{2}$ teaspoon white pepper
1 tablespoon finely chopped chives
40 g/1$\frac{1}{2}$ oz flour
1 litre/2 pints beef stock

Wash, drain and finely chop the bone marrow. Separate the eggs. Whisk the whites until stiff. Beat the egg yolks with the bone marrow, salt, pepper and chives. Fold the egg whites and flour into the mixture and, using a broad knife, spread thickly on a baking sheet. Cook in a moderate oven (180 C, 350 F, gas 4) for about 20 minutes until solidified. Meanwhile heat the stock. Cut the cooked marrow mixture into small squares or lozenge shapes and add to the hot stock just before serving.

Boiled beef

Tafelspitz

2.5 litres/4$\frac{1}{4}$ pints water
1.25 kg/2$\frac{1}{4}$ lb silverside or brisket of beef
1 teaspoon salt
2 carrots
$\frac{1}{2}$ celeriac
2 leeks
1 onion
$\frac{1}{2}$ teaspoon black pepper

Bring the water to the boil. Place the beef in the boiling water, add the salt and simmer over a low heat for 1$\frac{1}{2}$ hours. Cut the carrots into sticks. Thickly peel, wash and thinly slice the celeriac. Cut off the root end of the leeks, remove any coarse green leaves, cut into 5-cm/2-in lengths and then halve these. Wash and drain thoroughly. Add the carrot, celeriac and leek to the meat and continue simmering. Slice the onion. When the other vege-tables begin to soften add the onion and the black pepper to the meat. Test with a fork to see if the meat and vegetables are cooked and cut the meat against the grain into 1-cm/$\frac{1}{2}$-in slices. Arrange on a warm plate and surround with the vegetables.

Serve with: Spinach or cauliflower, potatoes boiled in stock and horseradish sauce (recipe below).

Horseradish sauce

Semmelkren

2 tablespoons freshly grated horseradish
300 ml/$\frac{1}{2}$ pint stock from the boiled beef
(Tafelspitz)
2 bread rolls
$\frac{1}{2}$ teaspoon salt
$\frac{1}{4}$ teaspoon sugar
1 teaspoon lemon juice
1 teaspoon cornflour
4 tablespoons double cream

Simmer the grated horseradish in the stock for 5 minutes. Meanwhile, remove the crust from the rolls, finely dice the bread, add to the stock and simmer for a further 5 minutes. Season the sauce with the salt, sugar and lemon juice. Stir the cornflour into the cream, pour into the sauce and bring to the boil, stirring continuously, until the sauce has thickened.

Wiener schnitzel

4 veal schnitzel, about 150 g/5 oz each
1 teaspoon salt
about 4 tablespoons flour
1 egg
1 tablespoon milk
1 teaspoon oil
100 g/4 oz dry breadcrumbs
75 g/3 oz butter for frying
Garnish:
4 sprigs parsley
4 slices lemon

Flatten the schnitzel with the ball of your hand to a uniform thickness of 3–5 mm/$\frac{1}{8}$–$\frac{1}{4}$ in. Lightly salt on both sides and coat in flour. Beat the egg with the milk and oil and coat the schnitzel in the egg mixture. Allow any excess to drip off and then coat in breadcrumbs. Do not press the crumbs on with your fingers but lightly press each side of the schnitzel and shake off any excess crumbs. Heat the butter in a large frying pan. Place the schnitzel one after the other in the hot fat and fry for about 2 minutes until golden on one side, then turn and fry on the second side for 4 to 5 minutes. Keep the schnitzel separate in the pan as they fry. Drain the schnitzel on paper serviettes and garnish with a little parsley and a slice of lemon.

Serve with: Green salad or potato salad. Otherwise, parsleyed new potatoes and lightly cooked fresh vegetables are a good accompaniment to this dish. Use whatever vegetables are in season.

Wiener schnitzel

Cherry strudel

Kirschenstrudel

1 egg
generous pinch of salt
6 tablespoons lukewarm water
175 g/6 oz butter, melted
225 g/8 oz flour
1 kg/2 lb morello cherries
100 g/4 oz breadcrumbs
5 tablespoons sugar
icing sugar for dusting

Beat the egg with the salt and water. Add 1 tablespoon of the melted butter to the egg mixture and gradually work this mixture into the flour. Knead the dough until smooth, then cover and leave to rest for 1 hour. Wash, stone and drain the cherries.

Spread a tea-towel on the worktop and sprinkle with flour. Place the dough on the cloth and roll out until thin. Then carefully stretch the rolled dough over the back of your hand until paper-thin. You will have to be very careful to avoid tearing the pastry. Cut off the thicker edges. Stir the breadcrumbs into half the remaining melted butter. Spread this mixture over two-thirds of the pastry. Top with the cherries and sprinkle with the sugar. Brush most of the remaining melted butter over the uncovered part of the pastry. Starting at the narrow side of the pastry, roll up the strudel by lifting the tea-towel and shape into a uniform roll. Brush the top with the rest of the melted butter. Transfer the strudel to a greased baking sheet and bake in a moderately hot oven (200 C, 400 F, gas 6) for about 40 minutes. When cooked sprinkle with icing sugar.

Variation: You can use the same pastry to make Viennese apple strudel. For the filling you will need: 675 g/1½ lb thinly sliced apple, 1 tablespoon rum, 4 tablespoons sugar, generous pinch of ground cinnamon, 2 tablespoons ground almonds and 50 g/2 oz raisins.

Kaiser pancakes

Kaiserschmarrn

5 eggs
450 ml/¾ pint single cream
150 g/5 oz flour
pinch of salt
fat for frying
sifted icing sugar for dusting

Separate the eggs. Beat the cream with the yolks, flour and salt. Leave to stand for 10 minutes. Whisk the egg whites until stiff and fold into the mixture. Using a little fat in a frying pan, fry small pancakes and, after turning them when the mixture has solidified, break into small pieces using 2 forks. Then continue frying until golden brown. Sprinkle with the sifted icing sugar before serving.

Serve with: Bilberries or other stewed fruit.

Kaiser pancakes

Cherry strudel

41

Hungary

Hungarian goulash

Tokány

50 g/2 oz streaky bacon
225 g/8 oz braising steak
225 g/8 oz lean veal
225 g/8 oz lean pork
3 green peppers
3 onions
4 tomatoes
50 g/2 oz fat (lard or oil)
1 tablespoon sweet paprika
1 teaspoon salt
600 ml/1 pint beef stock
2 teaspoons flour
150 ml/¼ pint soured cream

Chop the bacon. Cut the meat into bite-sized pieces. Halve the peppers, remove the seeds and pith and cut into strips. Dice the onions and the tomatoes.

Heat the bacon in the fat in a stewpan. Add the onion and fry until transparent. Add the meat and sprinkle with the paprika and salt. Stir in the strips of pepper, then the stock. Cover the pan and cook over a moderate heat for 30 minutes. Add the tomatoes and continue cooking until all the meat is tender – about 1½ hours. Add a little more stock as and when necessary. At the end of the cooking time stir the flour into the cream and use to thicken the stew.

Chicken paprika

Csirkepaprikás

2 tablespoons oil
4 chicken portions
1 large onion, chopped
1 clove garlic, crushed
1 tablespoon sweet paprika
250 ml/8 fl/oz chicken stock
3–4 tablespoons soured cream
salt and freshly ground pepper

Heat the oil in a large frying pan and brown the chicken pieces all over. Remove from the pan and reserve. Add the onion and garlic to the pan and fry for a couple of minutes before adding the paprika and chicken stock. Return the chicken portions to the pan, cover and simmer for about 30 minutes over a gentle heat. Stir in the soured cream and season to taste with salt and pepper.

Paprika vegetables

450 g/1 lb tomatoes
450 g/1 lb green peppers
75 g/3 oz rindless bacon
1 large onion, chopped
2 teaspoons sweet paprika
salt and freshly ground black pepper

Peel the tomatoes as described on page 7, then quarter. Halve and deseed the peppers, removing any pith, and cut into strips. Dice the bacon and dry fry in a heavy based pan. Add the onion and cook for a further few minutes before adding the pepper. Cook for 5 minutes then add the tomatoes and paprika. Season to taste with salt and pepper then simmer gently for 30 minutes, stirring occasionally.

Hungarian goulash

Middle East and Africa

Stuffed aubergines

Imam bayildi – Turkey

4 medium aubergines
3 tablespoons oil
3 onions
450 g/1 lb tomatoes
3 cloves garlic
½ teaspoon salt
pinch of white pepper
1 bay leaf
1 piece cinnamon stick
4 tablespoons finely chopped parsley
Garnish:
6 anchovy fillets
12 black olives

Cut the stalk end off the aubergines. Heat 2 tablespoons oil in a frying pan and fry the aubergines for 5 minutes, turning from time to time. Carefully skin the aubergines then halve lengthways and hollow out enough of the centre to allow for stuffing but not so much as to make them collapse. Cut the onions into thin rings. Peel the tomatoes (see page 7) and chop. Heat the remaining oil in the frying pan and fry the onions until golden brown. Add the tomatoes, cover the pan and cook for 5 minutes. Crush the garlic then add to the tomatoes with the salt, pepper, bay leaf, cinnamon stick and parsley and cook for a further 10 minutes. Remove the bay leaf and cinnamon stick. Place the aubergine halves in a greased baking dish, fill with the vegetables and bake in a moderate oven (180C, 350F, gas 4) for 15 to 20 minutes. Halve the anchovy fillets lengthways. Garnish the aubergines with anchovy rings and olives.

Stuffed aubergines

Lamb rissoles

Kofta – North Africa

2 onions
4 tablespoons oil
450 g/1 lb lean minced lamb
1 teaspoon salt
¼ teaspoon cayenne
pinch of ground cinnamon
1 egg
breadcrumbs, as required

Finely chop the onions and fry in 2 tablespoons oil until golden brown. Work the fried onion into the minced lamb with the salt, cayenne, ground cinnamon and egg. If necessary add breadcrumbs to give a workable consistency. Heat the grill. Shape the mixture into 4-cm/2½-in balls, lightly flatten and brush with oil. Place the rissoles on the oiled rack of a barbecue or grill and cook for about 5 minutes each side.

Burghul tomato salad

Tabbouleh – Arabia

100 g/4 oz burghul (cracked wheat)
450 g/1 lb tomatoes
2 onions
2 sprigs parsley and a few lemon balm leaves
2 tablespoons chopped fresh mint
1 teaspoon salt
pinch of white pepper
3 tablespoons lemon juice
6 tablespoons olive oil

Soak the burghul in water for 45 minutes. Then pour into a sieve lined with muslin, drain and then squeeze out in the cloth.

Thinly slice the tomatoes and finely chop the onions. Wash, drain and finely chop the parsley and lemon balm. Mix the herbs with the salt, pepper, lemon juice and oil to make a dressing. Mix into the burghul and tomatoes and leave the salad to stand for 10 minutes.

Okra and mince bake

Bamia – Egypt

675 g/1½ lb fresh or canned okra
1 onion
6 tomatoes
1–2 cloves garlic
6 tablespoons oil
450 g/1 lb minced beef
1 teaspoon salt
300 ml/½ pint beef stock
3 tablespoons natural yogurt
3 tablespoons soured cream
½ teaspoon pepper
Garnish:
lemon slices
tomato slices

Wash fresh okra thoroughly, then drain and cut off stalks. Halve large okra. If using canned okra drain and, if preserved in tomato juice, keep the juice. Finely chop the onion. Peel the tomatoes (see page 7) and finely chop. If you have tomato juice from tinned okra then 2 tomatoes will be sufficient, otherwise use the quantity given above. Crush the garlic. In a saucepan heat 3 tablespoons oil, add the okra and fry for 6 minutes, stirring from time to time. Remove from the pan and drain. Pour the fat out of the pan. In the pan heat 2 more tablespoons oil and fry the onion and tomato for 2 to 3 minutes, stirring from time to time. Add the mince and fry until brown all over. Add the salt, garlic, stock and, if you have it, the tomato juice and cook until almost all the liquid has evaporated. Stir together the yogurt, cream and pepper, then add to the meat. Grease a deep baking dish with oil and cover the base with half the minced meat. Smooth down, cover with the okra and top with the remaining meat. Sprinkle the top with a little oil and bake in a moderate oven (180 C, 350 F, gas 4) for 50 to 60 minutes. If the top becomes dry during baking sprinkle with a few spoons of hot water or stock. Garnish the okra bake with lemon and tomato slices.

Serve with: Pitta bread.

Noodle stew

East Africa

450 g/1 lb pork fillet
1 tablespoon oil
2 onions, diced
3 tomatoes
1 clove garlic, crushed
salt and pepper
1 chilli
2 teaspoons lemon juice
2 teaspoons sugar
2 teaspoons Worcestershire sauce
350 g/12 oz ribbon noodles
100 g/4 oz Cheddar cheese, grated

Cut the meat into 2.5-cm/1-in cubes. Heat the oil and fry the onion and meat. Peel and chop the tomatoes (see page 7) and add to the pan. Mix the crushed garlic with a little salt and add to the meat mixture. Halve the chilli, deseed, slice very thinly and add to the pan.

Season the mixture with the lemon juice, sugar, Worcestershire sauce, salt and pepper. Cover and cook over a gentle heat for about 30 minutes.

Meanwhile, cook the noodles in plenty of boiling, salted water for about 6 to 8 minutes, until 'al dente' (just done). Stir the cooked, drained noodles into the meat mixture and add the cheese.

Okra and mince bake

Stuffed turkey

United States

1 small turkey, about 4 kg/9 lb
3 teaspoons salt
1½ teaspoons white pepper
½ teaspoon dried thyme
450 g/1 lb canned chestnuts
1 head celery
100 g/4 oz butter
pinch of ground mace
3 tablespoons hot chicken stock
1 tablespoon single cream
2 tablespoons finely chopped parsley

Remove the giblets from inside the turkey. Wash the turkey well inside and out and wipe dry. Rub inside and out with 2 teaspoons salt, 1 teaspoon pepper and the thyme. Drain the chestnuts. Wash and finely chop the celery.

Heat 4 tablespoons butter in a pan. Add the chestnuts, celery, scant 1 teaspoon salt, ½ teaspoon pepper, the mace and stock, cover the pan and cook for 10 minutes, stirring from time to time. If you like you can add the finely chopped turkey liver for the last 2 minutes. Mash the mixture to a paste or strain through a sieve then add the cream and parsley. Stuff the turkey with the mixture and sew up the body cavity. Tie the legs and wings in to the body. Place the turkey, breast uppermost, in a roasting tin. Melt the remaining butter and pour over the turkey. Place the tin in the bottom shelf of a moderately hot oven (190 C, 375 F, gas 5) for about 3 hours, basting from time to time with the juices in the pan. About 10 minutes before the end of the cooking time turn the oven up to very hot (240 C, 475 F, gas 9). The turkey is cooked when the juice runs clear and golden when you prick a leg with a fork.

To serve: Turn off the oven and leave the turkey in the oven for 10 minutes before carving. Divide the stuffing into portions and serve the roasting juices as a gravy.

Serve with: Sweetcorn, sweet potatoes and assorted salads.

Stuffed turkey

Boston-style baked beans

United States

450 g/1 lb dried haricot beans
350 g/12 oz smoked pork
2 tablespoons maple or golden syrup
1½ teaspoons mustard powder
½ teaspoon salt
½ teaspoon Worcestershire sauce
2 onions
2 cloves
50 g/2 oz thin rashers streaky bacon
2 tablespoons finely chopped parsley

Cover the beans with water and soak overnight. Boil the beans in the soaking water for about 1½ hours, making sure that they are covered with water throughout. Add the meat for the last 30 minutes. Drain the beans. Stir 600 ml/1 pint cooking water with the syrup, mustard powder, salt and Worcestershire sauce. Finely dice the meat. Chop 1 onion and stick the cloves into the other. Use an ovenproof casserole with a firmly fitting lid and line with the bacon rashers. Place the onion with the cloves in the casserole. Mix the beans with the chopped meat and onion, tranfer to the casserole and pour on the sauce. Cover the casserole and bake in a moderate oven (180 C, 350 F, gas 4) for 1 hour. Then remove the lid and bake for a further 30 minutes to brown. Sprinkle with the parsley and serve from the casserole.

Boston-style baked beans

Fried scampi

United States

8 large frozen peeled scampi
2 tablespoons pineapple juice (from can)
$\frac{1}{4}$ teaspoon salt
pinch of cayenne
4 slices canned pineapple
50 g/2 oz butter
1 tablespoon brandy

Sprinkle the scampi with the pineapple juice, salt and cayenne, cover and leave to defrost.

Halve the pineapple slices and warm the butter in a frying pan. Drain the scampi and brown in the butter. Add the pineapple and warm through. Stir in the scampi marinade and the brandy and serve immediately.

Chicken king

United States

1 green pepper
1 red pepper
150 g/5 oz button mushrooms
50 g/2 oz butter
575 g/1¼ lb cooked chicken breast, boned and skinned
salt and white pepper
300 ml/½ pint single cream
½ teaspoon paprika
2 egg yolks
4 tablespoons dry sherry
1 tablespoon brandy

Halve the peppers, remove the seeds and pith, wash and cut into narrow strips. Trim, clean and slice the mushrooms. Heat the butter in a saucepan. Add the peppers, cover the pan and simmer over a low heat for 10 minutes. Then add the mushrooms and cook for a further 5 to 10 minutes. Thinly slice the chicken breast, season to taste and warm through in the cream. Add the vegetables. Sprinkle on the paprika and stir in. Beat the egg yolks with the sherry and brandy. Remove the pan from the heat and thicken with the egg mixture. Do not allow the mixture to boil from this point on.

To serve: Serve the Chicken king over a spirit lamp at the table, or on toast.

Cook's tips: If you want to freeze Chicken king do not add the last three ingredients. Wait until defrosted and reheated before adding the egg mixture.

Trout with bacon

Truite étuvée – Canada

4 medium trout, gutted
2 teaspoons lemon juice
½ teaspoon salt
generous pinch of white pepper
3 tablespoons butter
225 g/8 oz thin rashers lean bacon
300 ml/½ pint soured cream to serve

Wash the trout inside and out and pat dry. Rub inside with the lemon juice, salt and pepper. Grease a large baking dish with a lid with the butter and line with half the bacon rashers. Place the trout in the dish and cover with the remaining bacon. Place the lid on the dish and bake in a moderate oven (180 C, 350 F, gas 4) for 30 to 40 minutes. Then remove the lid and cook for a further 5 minutes to brown.

To serve: Serve from the dish with the soured cream as a sauce.

Cook's tip: Alternatively the trout can be baked in aluminium foil.

Fried scampi

Stuffed corn pancakes

Enchiladas – Mexico

100 g/4 oz flour
4 tablespoons cornflour
4 eggs
5 tablespoons oil
¾ teaspoon salt
4 tomatoes
1 red pepper   2 chillies
350 g/12 oz cooked chicken
8 green olives, stoned
1 onion   1 clove garlic
1 tablespoon finely chopped parsley
2 tablespoons ground almonds
6 tablespoons milk
1 teaspoon paprika
pinch each of pepper and chilli powder
1 tablespoon grated Cheddar cheese

Make a smooth pancake batter from the flour, cornflour, 3 eggs, 2 teaspoons oil, ¼ teaspoon salt and a little water. Leave to stand for 10 minutes. Peel and chop the tomatoes (see page 7). Remove the stalks, pith and seeds from the pepper and chillies and finely chop. Dice the chicken and olives. Finely chop the onion and garlic. Heat 1 tablespoon oil and fry the onion and garlic until transparent. Add the tomatoes, peppers and chillies. Add ½ teaspoon salt, the parsley and a little water if necessary and cook over a low heat to give a thick paste. Meanwhile use most of the remaining oil to fry thin pancakes from the batter and keep hot. Add the chicken, olives and ground almonds to the vegetable mixture and warm through. Beat the remaining egg with the milk, paprika, pepper and chilli powder. Dip the pancakes both sides in this mixture one after the other and re-fry in a little oil. Fill with the meat and vegetable mixture, roll up and sprinkle with the cheese.

Stuffed corn pancakes

Creole shellfish soup

Gumbo – Brazil

1 onion
½ red pepper
4 tomatoes
3 tablespoons butter
1 clove garlic, crushed
1 litre/2 pints chicken stock
100 g/4 oz canned chick peas
½ bay leaf
pinch of dried tarragon
salt and freshly ground white pepper
225 g/8 oz peeled cooked prawns, defrosted if frozen
8–10 canned or frozen mussels, drained or defrosted
100 g/4 oz canned crabmeat
1 teaspoon lemon juice
generous pinch of cayenne

Finely chop the onion. Remove the seeds and pith from the red pepper, then wash and finely chop. Finely chop the tomatoes. Melt the butter in a large pan and fry the onion, garlic and red pepper for 5 minutes without allowing them to brown. Add the chicken stock then add the chick peas, tomato, bay leaf and tarragon and season to taste. Cook over a low heat for 15 minutes. Then add the prawns and mussels. Allow to heat through in the soup then add the flaked crabmeat. Heat for a further 5 minutes and then season with lemon juice and plenty of cayenne.

Chicken in nut sauce

Pollo en nojada – Mexico

1 oven-ready chicken, about 1.5 kg/3½ lb
4 tablespoons lard or oil
1 teaspoon salt
1 onion
1 clove garlic
1 tablespoon breadcrumbs
100 g/4 oz pecan or walnuts, finely chopped
100 g/4 oz peanuts, finely chopped
¼ teaspoon pepper
pinch of ground cloves

Wash the chicken inside and out, wipe dry and cut into portions. Heat 2 tablespoons lard or oil in a saucepan and fry the chicken pieces over a high heat until golden brown. Add sufficient water to just cover the chicken and ½ teaspoon salt. Cover the pan and cook over a moderate heat for 30 minutes.

Finely chop the onion and garlic. Heat the remaining lard in a saucepan and fry the onion and garlic until transparent. Add the breadcrumbs and nuts. Stir in 600 ml/1 pint of the chicken cooking liquid and simmer gently for 5 minutes. Season this sauce with the pepper, cloves and the remaining salt to taste. Add the chicken pieces to the sauce and cook for a further 10 minutes over a low heat.

Serve with: Boiled or baked jacket potatoes and a crisp green salad.

Beef in lemon sauce

Thailand

1 kg/2 lb braising steak
1 large and 5 small onions
3 chillies
juice of 3 lemons
a few slices of fresh root ginger or 1 teaspoon
ground ginger
1 teaspoon salt
3 cloves garlic
4 tablespoons oil
300 ml/½ pint beef stock
8 tomatoes

Cut the meat into cubes. Chop the large onion. Remove stalks and seeds from the chillies and then chop. Mix the chopped onion and chillies with the lemon juice, ginger and salt. Pour over the meat and marinate overnight.

Finely chop the small onions and the garlic. Heat the oil. Fry the onion and garlic until transparent.

Add the meat and marinade. Add a little stock as necessary and braise for 1½ to 2 hours, or until the meat is tender. Peel the tomatoes (see page 7), remove the seeds and dice the flesh. Add the tomatoes to the meat shortly before the end of the cooking time and heat through with the meat.

Serve with: Plain boiled rice sprinkled with finely chopped coriander leaves.

Beef in lemon sauce

Chicken soup

Soto ajam – Indonesia

1 oven-ready boiling fowl, about 1.5 kg/3½ lb
4 onions
2 litres/3½ pints water
1 teaspoon salt
2 eggs
1 tablespoon oil
100 g/4 oz celeriac, cut into thin strips
50 g/2 oz carrot, cut into fine strips
3 tablespoons finely chopped fresh root ginger
½ teaspoon white pepper
5 tablespoons dry sherry
100 g/4 oz bean sprouts
2 teaspoons cornflour

Wash the fowl inside and out. Cut two of the onions in half and two into slices. Bring the water to the boil with the salt and onion halves. Add the chicken and boil for 1 hour. Hard boil the eggs for 10 minutes, plunge into cold water and shell.

Lift the chicken out of the stock, bone it and cut the meat into bite-sized pieces. Heat the oil and quickly fry the strips of celeriac and carrot. Strain the chicken stock, then reheat. Add the strips of vegetable, root ginger and white pepper. Stir the sherry into the bean sprouts. Dissolve the cornflour in a little water and use to slightly thicken the soup. Dice the eggs and add to the soup with the chicken and bean sprouts.

Fried rice

Nasi goreng – Indonesia

225 g/8 oz long-grain rice
1.5 litre/2¾ pints water
1½ teaspoons salt
100 g/4 oz peeled cooked prawns, defrosted if frozen
100 g/4 oz canned crabmeat
225 g/8 oz cooked chicken, boned and skinned
3 small onions
1 clove garlic
150 ml/¼ pint oil
1 small red pepper
1 tablespoon curry powder
2 tablespoons finely chopped parsley

Wash the rice until the water runs clear. Bring the water to the boil with the salt. Add the rice and boil in the open pan over a moderate heat for 12 to 15 minutes. Drain the rice in a sieve, rinse with lukewarm water, drain again, return to the empty pan and stir over a low heat for about 2 minutes until dry.

Rinse the prawns and crabmeat, drain and remove any tough fibres from the crab. Cut the chicken into narrow strips. Chop the onions and crush the garlic.

Heat the oil in a large saucepan and fry the onion and garlic over a low heat until transparent. Remove the seeds and pith from the red pepper, chop then add to the onion, fry for a few minutes and then stir in the curry powder. After a few minutes add the chicken and rice, season with salt and fry for a further 10 minutes, stirring frequently. Finally add the prawns and crabmeat and heat through. Pile the fried rice onto a serving plate and sprinkle with the parsley.

Serve with: Sambal oelek, chilli sauce, gherkins, mixed pickles, bottled peppers, mango and tomato chutney, fried banana, pineapple and tomatoes, toasted flaked coconut – and preferably as many of these as you have.

Fried rice

East Asia

Peking duck
Pei-ching-k'ao-ya – China

1 oven-ready duck, about 2 kg/4½ lb
10 spring onions with leaves
2 tablespoons honey
1 teaspoon ground ginger
150 ml/¼ pint cold water
2½ teaspoons salt
150 g/5 oz flour
6 tablespoons boiling water
1 tablespoon oil
2 tablespoons soy sauce to serve

Wash the duck inside and out and wipe dry very thoroughly. Cut the leaves off 2 spring onions and reserve. Peel and finely chop the white, then bring to the boil with the honey, ginger and cold water.

Rub the inside of the duck with 2 teaspoons salt, fill with the leaves from the 2 onions and sew up the opening. Brush the duck all over with the boiling honey mixture and hang for 12 hours in a well ventilated place to allow the skin to dry out.

Place the duck, breast side uppermost, on a roasting rack and roast for 1 hour in a moderately hot oven (190 C, 375 F, gas 5) for 1 hour. Meanwhile sift the flour into a mixing bowl, add the boiling water and ½ teaspoon salt and work in to make a smooth dough. Roll out the dough, cut into small rounds and roll these out until extremely thin. Heat the oil with 2 tablespoons water in a frying pan with a lid and cook the pancake rounds in the covered pan for 20 minutes. After 1 hour turn the duck over and roast in a hot oven (220 C, 425 F, gas 7) for a further 15 to 20 minutes until brown and crisp. Thinly slice the remaining onions with their leaves.

To serve: Joint the duck, remove the skin and cut the duck into bite-sized pieces. First you eat the skin and the meat with the sliced spring onion which should be sprinkled with soy sauce and wrapped in the pancakes.

Peking duck

Grilled eel kebabs
Unagi-kabayaki – Japan

1 fresh eel, about 1 kg/2 lb
250 ml/8 fl oz rice wine (sake) or dry sherry
3 tablespoons soy sauce
1 tablespoon honey
pinch each of cayenne and salt
1 teaspoon lemon juice
1 tablespoon oil

Get your fishmonger to skin and fillet the eel. Wash the fillets and cut into 2.5-cm/1-in lengths. Warm the rice wine or sherry with the soy sauce, honey, cayenne and salt. Sprinkle the eel pieces with the lemon juice, pour on the marinade and leave for 15 minutes.

Drain the eel and thread onto skewers. Cook in the grill pan with the oil or on an oiled grill rack for about 15 minutes, turning frequently and brushing repeatedly with the marinade.

Chicken with walnuts
China

450 g/1 lb chicken, boned and skinned
2 tablespoons soy sauce
2 tablespoons dry sherry
pinch each of pepper and sugar
2 teaspoons finely chopped root ginger
100 g/4 oz walnuts
2 shallots
3 tablespoons oil
6 tablespoons water or chicken stock
½ teaspoon salt

Cut the chicken into narrow strips about 2.5 cm/1 in long. Mix the soy sauce with the sherry, pepper, sugar and ginger, then marinate the chicken for 15 minutes. Halve the walnuts. Peel and slice the shallots. Heat the oil in a deep pan. Fry the shallots until transparent but not brown. Add the chicken with its marinade and stir over a high heat for 2 minutes. Add the water or stock, the nuts and salt (if using stock add only a pinch of salt) and gently cook for a further 5 minutes.

Mongolian soup

1 kg/2 lb lean lamb (leg, shoulder or
boned cutlets)
75 g/3 oz glass noodles
2 leeks
225 g/8 oz celery
225 g/8 oz mushrooms
6 uncooked oysters
6 tablespoons soy sauce
1 tablespoon honey
2 egg yolks
2 tablespoons rice wine (sake) or dry sherry
2 litres/3½ pints lamb or chicken stock
1 tablespoon finely chopped parsley
1 tablespoon finely chopped shallot
pinch of ground ginger
½ clove garlic, crushed

Get your butcher to cut the lamb into very thin
slices. If you are going to slice it yourself first chill it
for 2 hours in the freezer. Cut the slices into 5-cm/
2-in squares. Cover the noodles with hot water and
soak for 20 minutes. Trim and wash the leeks,
celery and mushrooms. Cut the leeks and celery
into strips and the mushrooms into thin slices.
Wash and open the oysters, remove from the shells
and drain. Drain the noodles.

Beat the soy sauce with the honey, egg yolks and
rice wine or sherry. Place the meat, noodles,
vegetables, oysters and sauce in separate dishes.
Heat the meat or chicken stock in an enamel or
metal fondue pot. Authentic Mongolian pans had
a holder in the centre for hot charcoal or a spirit
lamp. The stock is kept hot at the table over a spirit
lamp. Add the parsley, shallot, ground ginger and
crushed garlic to the stock.

To serve: Place the fondue pot in the middle of the
table. Cook the pieces of meat individually in the
stock on skewers or fondue forks and dip in the
sauce to cool. Eventually add the oysters, vegetables and noodles to the stock, cook for 2 minutes
and serve as a soup.

Liver in sesame sauce

Kan chupsi – Korea

450 g/1 lb calves' liver
2 spring onions with leaves
4 tablespoons oil
½ clove garlic, crushed
2 tablespoons sesame seeds
150 ml/¼ pint water
2 teaspoons cornflour
1 tablespoon soy sauce
pinch of salt
pinch of sugar

Wipe the liver dry and cut into fingers. Thinly slice
the spring onions with the tender leaves. Heat the
oil in a frying pan. Quickly fry the spring onion,
garlic and sesame seeds. Add the liver and stir for 2
to 3 minutes then add the water. Dissolve the
cornflour in a little water and use to thicken the
gravy. Remove the pan from the heat. Add the soy
sauce, salt and sugar, season to taste and serve
immediately.

Mongolian soup

Prawns in batter

Tempura – Japan

a small piece fresh root ginger
2 tablespoons soy sauce
2 tablespoons rice wine (sake)
150 ml/¼ pint water or stock
1 teaspoon ginger wine
2 eggs
1 teaspoon oil
100 g/4 oz flour
50 g/2 oz rice flour
1 white radish (mooli)
oil or vegetable fat for deep frying
450 g/1 lb peeled cooked prawns, defrosted if
frozen

Finely chop the root ginger. Bring the soy sauce to
the boil with the rice wine, water or stock, chopped
ginger and ginger wine and then leave to cool.

Beat the eggs with the oil, the flour, rice flour and a
little water to make a thick batter and leave to
stand for 10 minutes.

Peel and grate the radish. Heat the oil or vegetable
fat. Dip the prawns in the batter and deep-fry.
Drain well and serve hot.

To serve: Divide the prawns into individual
bowls. In separate bowls serve the radish mixed
with the soy sauce mixture. The prawns are given
extra flavour by dipping into the dish of radish.

Cook's tip: If preferred the prawns can be deep
fried at the table as for a fondue. The same recipe
can be used with pieces of fish instead of prawns,
together with vegetables such as carrot or bamboo
shoots.

Prawns in batter

Index